To Bar

it should have needed a new HYL stunt.

BILL *of* RITES *for* THE AMERICAN MAN

by K. COOPER RAY

Enjoy —

[signature]

Volume II

Illustrations by Victoria Molinelli

For my Father

Welcome. Please Come in.

SOCIAL PRIMER

CHARLESTON

❧ A Note from K. Cooper Ray ☙
Creator of SocialPrimer.com

Thank you for reading *Bill of Rites for the American Man*, Volume II. After the release of Volume I, I was asked many times over if there could be another version, which was more, well, gift worthy. Ha. This is the polite way of saying "Hey Cooper, we like your little pamphlet on etiquette but the format, not so much." Well, we still aren't moving on up to the leather-bound, gold page version I dreamt about, but this volume is a little closer to the original intent. I wanted BOR to be a pocket guide to the good life. Literally a little book you could stuff into your blazer pocket -- or even your back pocket -- for quick reference. And to be clear, BOR was never meant to be precious. It was meant to be dog-eared, beat up, with pages torn out and taped to your mirror or given to an uncouth friend. Like the good life we all aspire to live, this little book should not be exclusive or pretentious.

So a word about the title. *Bill of Rites for the American Man*. Yes, it is clever, and yes, it is catchy, a real play on words to be sure. I have even considered changing it for Volume II to something like *How to be a Southern Gentleman*, or *Wisdom of a Charleston Dandy*, even *Social Primer*, but as we look around the landscape these two years later the original title seems more apt than ever. Yes, I write, design and live in Charleston, South Carolina and was born in the Heart of Dixie (Montgomery, Alabama) but we are all men of the world now. We travel for business, we move, we take on new regions, and are exposed to new cultures. We all share a few common traits. We all struggle with the rites of passage into manhood. We all want to be better men, better citizens, and yes, we are American. We should share a common knowledge of the ways of the civilized world with helpful guide posts through the rites of passage. And what are these rites of passage into manhood? First kiss, first kill, first drive, first suit, first vote, first drink, first hangover are just a few of the time-worn tests we face. And to be clear, the recent explosion of Bro/Frat Culture is leading young men to the wrong trough. When junior high school boys think they are "Too Frat to Care" the joke has gone way too far. It seems to me that we must re-discover Manhood 101 in this country. In this current climate, civility seems to have no value. Intelligence is mocked. To be a man is not to put down another. To be a man is not to devalue women or the less fortunate. To be a man is not to embrace willful ignorance. The age old wisdom that to those whom much is given much is expected is true. Aping the style of those of the so-called elite or popular is commendable when that style is generous, gracious, moral, ethical, compassionate and kind. But when that style is arrogant, exclusive, mean-spirited or cruel then we have lost our way. Aim for the better angels of our nature. Let us value intelligence, civility, kindness and above all humor. Nothing says well-rounded man more than a great sense of humor combined with wisdom. It was none other than founding father Benjamin Franklin who said, "He that falls in love with himself will have no rivals." Funny, yes. And smart.

To wit, I have been called an "Alabama dilettante" (by no less an authority than *The New York Times*). I have been called pretentious and most recently, "regal" (by UrbanDaddy.com) and I have even been called a "Purple-suited Poon

Hound" by a commenter on Gawker.com (in my defense, the blazer was blue. It just read purple in the photograph, but that's too much back story. Ask me about this one over a Scotch the next time we meet). All this is to say, I want to make one thing perfectly clear from the outset. Although I am descended from a fine southern family, I grew up in Opelika, Alabama firmly ensconced in the middle of the middle class. I did not dance in Cotillion and had never attended a debutant ball before this year. I am a proud product of the Alabama public school system, from first grade to B.A. I have lived an extraordinary life, so far, and have been very lucky to meet many interesting people, dined at very fancy tables and been a guest in some pretty spectacular houses around the globe. And, I will proudly say, I have arrived at this station in life on my own and without a single letter of introduction or family connection, I struck out solo for New York City and later, the world at large.

This isn't to imply that I have not benefitted from generous people along the way but as for some silver spoon or grand letter of recommendation to the good life, this did not happen. My trek was filled with land mines, and mistakes were made.

The prevailing mantra on socialprimer.com -- and now here in this guide -- is that one does not have to be rich to live the good life. My experience is proof that anyone can step into the good life without being born into it. The genesis of Social Primer began as an idea after leaving my beloved Dixieland and stomping around the world for business and leisure. In my travels and residencies in Brooklyn, Manhattan, Milan, Paris, London, Cape Cod, Los Angeles, and now Charleston, I have spent much time observing the world around me and there were some pretty incredible experiences and fascinating people along the way. I don't want to give the impression that I was huddled in a closet scribbling notes and indulging insecurities. Hardly. In fact, a few old friends reading this now are recalling more than a few boozy nights. "Honey, is this the same Cooper who grounded our boat in Charleston Harbor at three in the morning?"

In my own social climb I have failed as many tests of civility as I have passed. You see, I have always been a chameleon who can easily slip into any situation that interested or intrigued me. During these experiences, I am embarrassed to admit, I wasn't always the most well-mannered chap. But it was these experiences, my own and those I observed, that made me appreciate the stark differences in how people behaved. From European royalty to members of so-called high society, I was, and remain, a close observer taking notes -- particularly of the men -- as I want nothing more than to measure up and fit in.

The mission of Social Primer evolved into a quest to open the door to the good life for others, to let us all in to enjoy that civilized life and eat at that fancy table. I want to break down the walls of exclusivity by instilling an unshakeable confidence so that men will feel at home wherever we may roam. We should never turn down an invitation to an event out of intimidation or fear of the unknown. Seize the day! Many of the rules listed throughout this primer were ingrained in me from an early age. Many more are gleaned from the pages of dusty old etiquette books. And finally there are the lessons I've learned from first-hand observation of so-called society people.

Do you know when to stand to greet a woman? Or when not to stand? Or perhaps you drink too much of the wrong liquor at a private dinner or onboard a beautiful sail boat and make an absolute fool of yourself ensuring you will never be invited back? (Ahem). Granted, there are times when the rituals of etiquette can seem archaic. The custom of a gentleman walking on the curbside of the street, for example, may in our harried times seem a ridiculous and antiquated notion and one less thing for a modern American man to worry about. But this seemingly outdated tradition – as well as all of the artucles illustrated in this primer – are important and are noticed by the women who expect this and the men who practice them. And yes, you will be judged if you don't know it, I won't judge you, but people will.

Cordially,

Most of the articles found in the Bill of Rites can be considered situational for everyday use but always ring true when we are in black-tie, at a business event or on a first date. This isn't to say that manners should be reserved for fancy and formal occasions. Everyday manners are the goal, but extra attention is paid to special events where the use of such is easier to illustrate for our purposes and crucial to execute when we are out on the town. Just as we want our dinner suit to be clean, pressed and ready for use when we need it, we should possess a confident grasp of the ways of the civilized world in our social lives.

Unfortunately, old-fashioned etiquette books are woefully dense with detail and many people, but particularly men, put them aside as not being relevant to our modern lives. Understandable but not insoluble. SP has delved deeply into these tomes and come away with an edited, updated and completely accessible set of articles that fit neatly into the modern American man's life. Stripped, pruned, updated and polished for your consideration, consider this a list of articles to the original declarations, a Bill of Rights, as it were. Or to take the pun further, a Bill of Rites, as in personal rites of passage for social confidence and success.

❧ Table of Contents ❧

The Articles

How to

A Man Stands

Article One: A Man Stands

*A Man Stands to Shake Hands or Dies
Trying: Keep Your Seat if You Want to
Repel Success and Make a Bad Impression*

Shaking Hands. My friend KDG was at a party recently where he ran into a man – we'll call this man Sam Snotwell -- with whom he was considering going into some business. As we approached Snotwell, my friend extended his hand to this prospective associate who was sitting insouciantly in his chair. Snotwell leaned back against the wall at a precarious angle and reluctantly extended his hand for a half-assed greeting. He did not even bother to put all four legs of the chair on the floor, and instead sat there leaning back against the wall like an insolent sloth. As we were leaving I advised my friend not to enter into any business with this cad for he obviously did not respect him. A few weeks later I read of Snotwell's indictment in the newspaper. The presence or absence of manners will tell you a lot about a man's character, for instance if he has any.

A man NEVER shakes hands sitting down. Never. Simple to say, simple to do. There is nothing more insulting than to be introduced to a man and the oaf refuses to stand to shake your hand. On the rare occasion that a man cannot offer his hand to shake or is out of reach, he would nod to acknowledge the greeting. If you are seated in a tight booth in a restaurant and rising to your feet would send the dinner plates flying, then rise slightly and, if within reach, shake the proffered hand. Otherwise, nod in the gentleman's direction and shake his hand when space and time allow. Out of respect, younger men should wait for an older man to extend his hand. If there is a large group of men being introduced to each other and the handshaking would become impossibly comic, a nod and "How do you, do?" will suffice. But if someone extends his hand you are required to shake it. Comedy be damned.

The instances just mentioned notwithstanding, I can think of no situation where a man of your own generation would not offer his hand to shake, especially upon the first introduction. But alas, there are ill-bred rogues whom we will encounter in our journey and in our role as non-apes, we will let it pass without comment, but not without observation.

❧ The Code ❧

☞ A man stands to shake hands.

☞ A man stands when someone his age or older enters a room. This applies to a woman, a man, a parent or a boss.

☞ A man stands for women and elders. It is the role of a gentleman to stand when greeting a woman or an elder and it is our small burden to bear. Admittedly, I have been in situations when a woman is coming and going from the table so often I can hardly make it through the meal or carry on a conversation attending to her, but nevertheless, it is right to stand up upon her leaving and her return. Now, God forbid, you are seated next to a party girl who is constantly popping up from the table to powder her nose with no regard for the company at the table, but again standing is the right thing to do. Her ill manners are no excuse to relax your own.

☞ A man stands when the woman seated to his right at the table rises to leave and when she returns. Nowadays few people adhere to the one-man-for-every-woman rule at table. In this case, you would rise for the woman next to you whether she is seated on the left or the right, especially if there is not a man on her left. You need not stand when the woman across from you comes and goes. That is her dinner partner's duty.

☞A man stands in a room in which any women are standing. The rules are relaxed these days in your workplace or on public transportation, but you would still give up your seat to a pregnant woman, an elderly man or woman or anyone who seems to be in distress or upset.

☞All men stand when a new woman approaches the table or the seat he is occupying. All men. I realize in this world of casual dinners and liberation it can seem awkward or dorky to rise from the table when a woman approaches, but it is correct and right.

☞When a woman rises from or returns to the table, the gentleman holds her chair and guides it under her.

25

❦ To that end, a note to the ladies. If you approach a table and you plan on lingering, do not allow the men to stand there waiting for you to sit down or move on. A gentle statement will set everything right. "Please take your seats, gentlemen," or a "Please don't get up," is all that is required and the gentlemen will be relieved and oblige. Although the old etiquette books tell men to ignore such a statement because if a woman really meant this she would not hover, in our modern times when many women have no clue about this courtesy you could be standing there all night while your Scotch gets warm and your steak gets cold. And that is the ultimate incivility in my book!

❦ For the record, a man never reaches to shake a woman's hand. If she offers, he certainly takes her hand but he does not initiate. Instead he politely nods his head in acknowledgment of the introduction. This is an old rule and one that can be difficult to manoeuvre in the modern world. If a woman in society or business extends her hand, you would surely take it, but the rule of civility is that a man would not aggressively reach for a woman. Perhaps this old rule applies only to women of a certain age and SP is admittedly a little old-fashioned. But this is correct, and I digress.

Say Your Name

Article Two: Say Your Name

Better to Be Remembered as John Smith than That Guy in the Funny Tie. Even C-3PO Had a Name. Say Yours When You Meet Someone.

One of the casualties of the instant-communication age is most felt in the art of introduction. How many times do you find yourself in this social (or business) situation? You are standing in a covey of people immersed in a rolling conversation when all at once you realize that you don't know the names of some of the people to whom you are talking. There is a queasy feeling of awkwardness rising in your chest, and you don't know how to correct the situation so you ride the roll through to the inevitable conclusion, parting ways without ever knowing who was who. There is an old saying — referring to a gathering in a private house — that says

"The roof constitutes an introduction," meaning you shouldn't introduce people in a private home. This is predicated on the assumption that the host has done his job and anyone under his roof should already be introduced to one another and to do so would be an insult to the host. This old rule was accepted in the days before the transportation revolution and familial displacement sent us all scurrying and gathering in far flung places. When your mothers were old acquaintances and all families and friends were well-known in a small community, this rule held true, and so it goes today. But we are a long way from cozy community living. We are citizens of the world. Let us always introduce ourselves.

❧ The Code ❧

☞ Say Your Name - In today's hurly burly society we have to pay extra attention to the small civilities. In the course of a conversation, it is never too late to say your name. But let's be clear.

You should say your name at the outset and expect the same courtesy of those you are meeting.

☞ Always use first and last names, mind you. It is annoying — not to mention ill-mannered — to introduce one person to another without saying both or more of the parties' names. This lapse is yet another casualty when we neglect to say someone's first and last name or worse mumble incoherently over the din in a crowded room. I know what you are thinking, but what if I don't know their last name when I make the introduction? It is not rude to ask someone their last name. Get this out of the way right at the beginning. If you've been introduced before and you've forgotten this is not a crime to ask again. Just don't make a habit of it. To habitually forget someone's name, first or last, is the height of incivility, the depth of laziness and in the end, just plain rude.
☞ Provide a Little Bio - On the other hand, you should always remind people

of your own name and even volunteer a little history of when you met. "I am Robert Hightower. We met at the Wilson's Christmas Party." This will assuage any awkwardness brewing inside the person whom you are greeting. And this person, in kind, should respond, "Of course I remember, Robert. It is good to see you again." No matter if this is true or not. The point of good manners is to make people feel at ease. Generosity is always the first rule of the day.

☞ Always say "How do you do?" or "It's great to see you." Never say "It's nice to meet you," unless you are absolutely certain you have never met before. In fact, you should simply remove this phrase from your social repertoire altogether and always say "It's nice to see you."

☞ Never say "Do you remember me?" This puts the other person in the awkward position of saying "No."

☞ Never announce a person's vocation in a social introduction as in "Do you know Jonathon from MGM?" In business, the opposite is true. If the gathering is business and social, then by all means include the vocation if it is relevant. Employ a little bio or shared interest to lay a little common ground between strangers. "Bill, this is my cousin James. He's from Montgomery. Don't you have family there?" or "Lucy, this is my co-worker Katherine. She's writing a book on internet start-ups. Didn't you just sell your company to Google?" The trick is to never force someone to resort to "How do you know each other?"

☞ Never put someone on pause that has come up to you to say hello. If you are so engrossed in a story with Helen Highwater that you feel compelled to ask Jasper Jones to hold while you finish, you should remove Mrs. Highwater to a private room — or go outside — so as not to be interrupted. Or better yet, call her the next day. Put yourself on pause, never Mr. Jones. This incident is far too common and exceedingly rude.

☞ On the other hand, Jasper Jones should not interrupt someone who is obviously engrossed in deep, gesticulating conversation. Although deep gesticulating conversation has no place at a drinks party, some people do engage in such. SP says keep it light and always be open to widening your circle. Isn't this why you attend these things in the first place?

❧ The Finer Points of Introductions ❧

Man defers to Woman as Younger
defers to Elder.

☞ As is the case with most of the rituals of etiquette, in the case of introductions, man defers to woman as younger defers to older or less distinguished to more so. Why is this the case? Simple respect. For example, if you would like to introduce your high school-aged cousin Elizabeth Hadaway to your mother's friend from her garden club, you would say, "Mrs. Highwater, may I present Elizabeth Hadaway?" Or, if "present" seems pretentious or formal, you might say, "Mrs. Highwater, I would like to introduce Elizabeth Hadaway." Or, if you are standing between the two of them you could say "Elizabeth Hadaway, Mrs. Highwater." Think of it as if you are gently handing the present of Elizabeth to the recipient Mrs. Highwater. The point here is that you are presenting the younger or less distinguished person to the older or more distinguished. The same would stand for gentlemen. "Mr. Highwater, may I present my cousin Charles Hadaway?"

☞ If the people are of the same age or generation, you would present the gentleman to the lady. "Mrs. Highwater, may I present Barton Bullweather?" Never say "Mr. Barton Bullweather." By his age and bearing, Mrs. Highwater will know he is a "mister".

☞ As for titles, there are exceptions to this rule, most notably in the cases of high-ranking officials or clergy. Just remember, introductions are based on respect. To that end, you would present your wife, girlfriend or boyfriend to your boss. "Mr. Wallingford, may I present my girlfriend, Julia Wannamaker."

☞ In everyday situations where the individuals are all the same age or generation, you would present the man to the woman: "Robert Johnson; Julia Wannamaker," or "I would like you to meet Robert Johnson." The thing to remember here is to always use given and surname (first and last).

☞ Never say Mister in front of your name. It is ridiculous and pretentious. The same goes for any title that is not official or clergy.

శ్రీ

The Art of Conversation

Article Three: The Art of Conversation

Everyone Has a Story to Tell. Just Don't Let Yours Be the Only One, Gas Bag.

One of the cornerstones in the foundation of good manners is Generosity. And this generosity extends to all areas of the civilized space, but never more so than in conversation. Admittedly, SP has a tendency to carry on and this is one rule that I catch myself breaking quite often. I can't help it. I really do like the sound of my voice, and my stories are generally more interesting than most. So when I catch myself growing hoarse from non-stop verbiage, I will remember Article Three and segue into a question to the obedient listener who has given me the gift of attention.

My own offense notwithstanding I ask you, is there anything more boring and frustrating than being held prisoner by a Conversation Hog? The CH is a person who is so enthralled by the sound of his own voice that he fills the empty space with his never-ending monologue. I recently attended a dinner party and found myself seated near a man of a certain age who upon first glance carried the bearing of a well-mannered man. His clothing was well-tailored and conservatively worn, his grooming was impeccable and his table manners exquisite. It was only through the course of the meal that his Achilles' heel was exposed to the company assembled. He began to tell a story and the story never ended.

Please don't misunderstand. The sharing of amusing anecdotes is as necessary to the success of a great dinner party as is a fork and a knife. A host expects his guests to entertain, enthrall and amuse his table. In fact, it is the duty of the well-received guest to provide such service. If a guest sat silently at any host's table without so much as the tiniest contribution to the evening's entertainment, this guest would not be invited back. Now on the other hand, enter the Conversation Hog who drones on and on without letting others at the table participate in the conversation. This particular gentleman – and I am being generous with that term for I particularly appreciated the cut of his jacket – began climbing the Everest of anecdotes, and the climb did not end. He meandered from inanity to inanity and barely took a breath in apparent fear of losing his grip. He reminded me of a child who doesn't want to share his toys with other children and holds them in a tight circle in his hands. This man went on a talking tour. He opened every side door and -- not content to provide a peek -- took his guest through every room then every book on the shelf, and even every nick on the table. Dull, I tell you, mind-numbingly dull. It was digression at its most egregious, and I wished there had been a pause button on his sleeve for I surely would have pressed it.

Generosity extends to everything we do, especially in conversation. The accomplished raconteur (and by his display of confidence, our CH certainly considered himself one) is one who reads his audience and edits his tale. Even if a storyteller lacks the smallest sense of humor, he should read the expression, the body language, the eyes of his audience, and if there is even the slightest sense of discomfort or glazing over he should wrap it up and wrap it up quick. I have heard many a host bemoan the greedy CH and vow to banish the villain from future guest lists. Do not a Conversation Hog be. It is as appalling as falling down drunk, and it is not valued in civilized company.

❧ The Code ❧

☞ Do not Interrupt - While the urge may pulse to interrupt the CH, this is the price of civilized company and (admittedly) the enabler for the phenomenon of conversation hogs. Caveat: SP is not one to sit idly by and let some buffoon steal the stage all of the time. In extreme cases, employ a little Guerilla Etiquette to take back a conversation which has been hijacked, but employ with caution.

☞ Keep it Clean - In mixed company, keep the topics bland until you know someone better. Mixed company means many things: mixed ages, mixed sexes, mixed socio/economic groups, what have you. The point being that the story you told your frat bros about throwing up in the parking lot the night before is not appropriate to retell once you have picked up your date or your parents and their friends. And while we're at it, let's just ban any words that describe body parts, body noises, sexual acts, or anything to do with things that come out of a body whether it's animal or human. Avoid curse words and vulgar expressions as well as slang. We aren't saying Yo, when we enter the civil arena. There's a word for this gentility of the tongue and it's called euphemism. Employ it.

For Example:

Vulgar Truth: Jason got so shitfaced last night I found him passed out next to the toilet this morning.

Civilized Euphemism: Jason got a little over-served last night and did not look his best this morning.

☞ Inventory Topics - Have a handy inventory of appropriate topics when you hit the civil circuit. These can be many things depending on your region and the event at hand. If you read the news, and I mean every day, you should be well-prepared for most conversations. Politics, unless you are a seriously balanced individual, should be avoided. Sports -- unless there is an extraordinary event happening at the time such as a World Series or a National Championship on the horizon -

- should not be the only topic in your arsenal.

❧ Handy Pre-Packaged Conversation Starters ❧

Where are you from? is much more interesting than What do you do? This question opens a giant conversational door revealing city, state, region, schools, arts and area interests.

How do you spend your days? is a great way of asking what someone does for a living without offending. Believe it or not, What do you do for a living? is a rude and impertinent question to ask a complete stranger. You may as well ask how much money he has in the bank and if he cheats on his taxes and his wife.

Handle Your Liquor

Article Four: Handle Your Liquor

or Your Liquor Will Handle You, and Not in a Good Way.

Now this subject rankles many, and it is the cause of quite a few heated (er, drunken) discussions. I realize that it takes some rather large cojones to tell a man what he should and should not drink. And don't think I haven't had my way up, down, around, inside and outside of a liquor cabinet. Hell, I opened a tavern for Pete's Sake; I know from which I speak. But please don't think I have not made some grave mistakes and lost many battles with the bottle. It wasn't like I wasn't warned at an early age. My father's advice when I left for college? "Son, drink Scotch indoors and Bourbon out." And he sent me on my way. If only I had listened to that sage advice I would have spent far fewer nights holding on to a spinning bed while begging and bargaining with

God to please make it stop. Not to mention the nights (and mornings) spent driving the proverbial porcelain bus. I think that's quite enough elucidation on that subject. We all have the horror stories; pick your own and insert here.

I will be the first to tell you that I love a booze hound. I would rather be with a good drinker than just about any other company. What could be more jovial, I ask you? Boozers, good boozers, are just about the happiest people on earth. I realize, believe me, there is a fine line between amiably tipsy and mean-spirited or sloppily drunk and over-served. Seriously, believe me. I'm not kidding. I know. I have one friend in particular who cannot judge his alcohol. The clinical diagnosis of this notwithstanding, let's just deal with the result. Every time he drinks, it is to get drunk. I said to him once, "You drink like a freshman." And it's true. We all have to learn the proper way to drink, and hopefully we learn by the time sophomore year rolls around. In my own boozy education, I have run the gamut from rum and coke (too sweet), to a gin and coke (a rookie move that made sense to a fraternity pledge) to classic Bourbon and coke (the staple of tailgating and football games) to every shot that ever curve-balled my way down a bar. I went through boozy boot camp for many years until finally arriving at this perfect social condition: I am, today, proud to announce that I am in excellent drinking shape. I know my body, my chemistry, my buzz. I can hang with the pros. Until I get cocky and fall off. Hey, it happens. I never said drinking was a perfect science. It's a mystical experience. I am something like a shaman. Trust me. So what did all this hard earned experience teach me? Taking into account every man's own personal chemistry, of course, we, over time, figure out what we can handle. In the hope of giving a novice a little head start or a Cliff's Notes boost, here's a little guide from a field-tested foot soldier in Jack Daniel's army.

One of my favorite quotes illustrates this philosophy perfectly: "Three juleps were his invariable number – either morning or evening. That amount of alcohol produced exactly the proper degree of philosophical detachment."

Dubose Heyward
(Peter Ashley)

❧ The Code ❧

☞ A man drinks Scotch. There is a reason Scotch has a reputation as the businessman's drink. You can drink copious amounts of Scotch and you will not fall down drunk, you will not make a fool of yourself in a public place and you will rarely have a hangover. It's true. Oh sure, your words will slur as they roll over your lips, but rest assured when you stick to Scotch you won't pick a fight (that's what Bourbon is for), you won't black out (Vodka) and you won't get mean or bitter (Gin).

☞ A man drinks Bourbon (see The Occasion & The Drink below).

☞ A man drinks a martini on occasion. But remember the rule: Two's not enough and three's too many.

☞ A man drinks beer with his bros, on the golf course, at the beach, camping in the woods, at a cookout, but never in black tie.

☞ A man drinks wine during dinner or when feeling reflective.

☞ A man does not drink cocktails. I abhor the word cocktails, just say "drinks."

☞ A man doesn't have a little umbrella sticking out of his Mai Tai because a man doesn't drink Mai Tais. Unless he's dining at Trader Vics, and I think even that fine old establishment has gone the way of the rotary telephone.

☞ A man doesn't drink White Russians, or any other frilly lady drinks designed to disguise the taste of alcohol. If you don't like the taste of alcohol (I can't believe this condition exists in any man) then just don't drink it. Order a club soda with a lime in it if you need to look cool and fit in.

☞ A man never drinks booze out of a straw.

☞ Forget the sweet stuff. Coca Cola and the like will make you sick. You don't need it. Just opt for club soda or seltzer (same thing). Exception: In stadiums Coke is usually the only choice and it's a tradition with Bourbon. NEVER mix scotch with Coke, Sprite, ginger ale or anything with flavor.

☞ A man drinks Champagne at a wedding, or when his girlfriend/boyfriend or wife pops a cork on a special occasion, but this is just that, a special occasion. A man should never, under any circumstance, drink a champagne cocktail.

☞ A man doesn't drink Jagermeister, or Goldschlager or any ridiculous concoction intended to make you wasted once he graduates from college. In fact, the Jager Bomb should be retired after junior year. Aren't you seeing the point here? A gentleman tries his damndest not to get wasted.

☞ If you've mastered your buzz with just the right amount of liquor and you take a hit on a bong, pipe or joint, all bets are off. You will throw up and pass out. Beware. Pot Heads and Booze Hounds don't really mix. These are two distinctly different milieus. Make a choice.

✥ Terms for ordering a drink ✥

Aperitif - French term for a light drink taken before a meal to stimulate appetite. I've never ordered this and don't really see the reason because Scotch stimulates my appetite just fine, thank you, but the word is bandied about often in conversation at fancy places and on fancy menus.

Back - an extra glass of something to accompany a drink. Bourbon on the rocks with a water back, is Bourbon on the rocks with a short glass of water.

Chaser - an extra glass of something to drink right after a liquor drink. Usually a shot with a beer chaser.

Highball - liquor served with ice, soda, water, ginger ale or carbonated liquids.

Neat - liquor that is drunk undiluted by ice, water or mixers at room temperature poured straight from the bottle. No ice.

Rocks - a beverage served over ice without adding water or other mixers.

Splash - a small amount of mixer added to a drink.

Straight Up - a drink chilled in a shaker and strained into a glass served up without ice.

Twist - lemon peel rubbed on the edge of a glass sometimes dropped into the drink

∂∞ What you get when ordering a drink at a bar ∞∂

Well - The cheapest liquor in the bar, sometimes called Rot Gut. This is what you get when you ask for a Scotch & soda, Vodka & Tonic, Bourbon & Coke. The cheapest price = the cheapest liquor.

Not a good idea. This is where the up-chuck comes from.

Call - The next level of quality liquor and price level. When you ask for the brand of liquor by name: Smirnoff & Tonic, Dewar's & Soda, Jim Beam & Coke.

Premium (or Top Shelf) - Highest price, quality and altitude (premium liquors sit on the top shelf). Ketel One & Tonic, Glenlivet on the rocks, Maker's Mark & Soda.

The Occasion…………………The Drink

Business mixer................. Scotch & Soda
Tailgate…………………Bourbon & Coke
Polo match…………...Champagne/Rosé
Clam bake…………………………….Beer
Oyster Roast...................................... Beer
Golf Course.. Beer
Club House.................................... Scotch
Poolside/Lawn Party…..…..Gin & Tonic
Gator Hunting................................... Beer
Grouse Shooting………...............Bourbon
Hangover…………...............Bloody Mary
Kentucky Derby.......................Mint Julep
Nascar Infield………...............Budweiser
Private Club................................... Scotch

Table Manners

Article Five: Table Manners

There's More to Eating than Shoveling Food from Plate to Mouth: When You're Out to Impress a Date, the Parents or the Boss, You Better Know How to Maneuver the Fork and Knife.

Table manners matter. Whether you are attending a formal dinner at the White House, a wedding reception in an exclusive club, a lunch or dinner in a restaurant, a fancy dinner party or just spending an evening with good friends gathering for a casual night in, manners matter. Whether you are trying to impress a girl, a boy, the parents, your boss or business associates, whomever, manners matter. People will notice these seemingly trifling things, and they will judge you. I won't, but people will. These snoots aren't as forgiving as I am because I want you to succeed. So stop moaning and listen up.

My friend SJM wrote to me the other day saying he witnessed a most unfortunate incident during a business lunch recently. At the table next to him was seated an older gentleman with a younger chap. By the nuggets of overheard conversation, the two were obviously engaged in an employment interview situation and it was Jack Youngman who was auditioning for the job. My friend says that Jack was well-dressed, articulate, and seemed to have a grasp of the occupation's vernacular and seemed well on his way to gainful employment.   Then the food was delivered. Now Jack did not fall victim to the usual booby traps. He'd placed his napkin in his lap. His utensils were all properly aligned. No, his was a trickier culprit. Chicken Salad. It seems Jack ordered the chicken salad sandwich and forgot that he wasn't at home or at his mom's house where it can be forgiven to have your food spill all about and then pick it up with your fingers. It's a sandwich, after all. It's called finger food. But, here's the tricky

66

part. Jack's chicken salad debacle was a distraction to the interviewer and in the end a distraction to his otherwise on-point performance.

I cannot tell you how many times I land at some schmancy restaurant and do little internal cartwheels when I see some juicy dish on the menu. Do you know how difficult it is to pass over a heaping helping of barbecue baby back ribs? But alas, I take a look at the person across from me and think, do they really want to see me sitting here with barbecue sauce smeared all over my face and hands? The same goes for the seemingly everyday burger. It can be a messy undertaking. Think about what you eat when you are trying to impress. When on a business lunch or first date, keep it simple and under the fork. That is, order something that you can cut into small bites and place easily into your mouth and chew without distraction. So no fried chicken, no unpeeled shrimp or lobster, no spaghetti or any long pasta you have to twirl and definitely no tacos or burritos. What, you ask, is the most business-appropriate lunch order? Well steak and a Scotch, of course. But if you don't plan to take a nap afterward, I would stick to a Caesar Salad, even a Cobb salad. Remember, you're not there to eat. You are there to impress. Don't blow it by eating like a ten-year-old. Sadly, I cannot report if Jack landed the job, but I hope so.

❧ The Code ❧

☞ When to begin. This seems to be one that many people are confused about. The one that says no one eats until all are served. This is simply not true. Once two have been served, you may begin. A friend of mine puts it thus, "When two have seats, all may eat." I don't know what the hell that means, but it does put people at ease, and rhymes are catchy and easy to remember.   You would, however, always wait for the hostess to be served. In restaurants, this can feel awkward as you wait for the food   to   come   out   together.   But nevertheless, you would be correct in eating. And your well-mannered companions should insist that you begin. Who wants to eat hot food cold? I take a lot of flack from the purist on this rule. As in all unfamiliar situations in life follow the leader. if you don't feel comfortable digging in until all are served, go ahead and wait until all are served. But do not judge those who begin, especially in a large party.

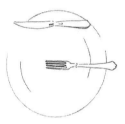

☞ During the meal, the fork should be placed in the middle of the plate with the handle to the right and just over the edge of the plate when not in use. The knife will rest at the top third of the plate with the handle and the knife point touching each edge of the plate. Never put a utensil on the table cloth once it has been used.

☞ Never leave a spoon in the soup bowl. When you have finished or are taking a break from the soup, place the spoon on a soup plate, or in the absence of such, on your main plate. To repeat, never put a used spoon on the table and do not leave it sitting in the bowl. Another fine point, when eating soup always push the spoon away from you, as in "the ship goes out to sea" not toward you. This is definitely an arcane piece of etiquette that I have no idea why or where this came from, but it's accepted and noticed.

☞ Your napkin stays in the seat of your chair if you leave the table during the meal. In fancy restaurants, the waiter will come by in your absence and refold the napkin and place it beside your plate. This annoys me a bit, but that's the way it goes. Never leave a dirty napkin on the table in sight of other dinner guests. When the meal is finished, place the napkin to the left of your plate – or in the center if the plate has been cleared. Do not refold it.

☞ Removing a bad bite. If you find something wrong with the bite in your mouth – gristle, bone, what have you – remove it the same way it went in: with your fork. It isn't easy. It isn't graceful. Just do it. And do it smoothly, quietly, unobtrusively, with no fuss. Wait until the conversation turns away from you and pull this maneuver as nonchalantly as possible. Return the food to your plate, disguised beneath the radishes so no one can see it. Do not spit it into your napkin unless there is some extreme reason, and if it's that extreme, excuse yourself.

☞ Bread is placed on the bread plate or main plate, torn by hand into bite size pieces and buttered one piece at a time. Butter is also place on the plate and used as needed.

A. 4:20   B. 3:15

☞ After the meal. When you have
finished eating place the fork and the
knife in the (A.) 4:20 position or (B.)
across the middle of the plate, parallel to
the edge of the table with the handles to
the right and flush with the edge of the
plate, not hanging over. Let's call this
one 3:15. Either way is correct. The fork
will be nearest you with the tines turned
up. The sharp side of the knife faces
down toward you. Why, you ask, is this
important? Because this simple
universal act signals to the staff, waiter
or otherwise, that you have finished
your meal. Then why is this important
when dining at home? Because practice
makes perfect, and this should become a
second nature habit. On the Continent
across the pond, the tines are turned
down at meal's end. SP once affected
this method — along with a couple of

other European rules — when I returned from a trip abroad while in high school. My aunt — a stickler for perfect table manners — stopped in mid-conversation to ask what I was doing. I replied that this was the way people did it in Europe. She responded with a terse, "Well, we are not in Europe." I have never strayed since.

☞ In business or on a date, once your interviewer (or your date) has selected the restaurant, find the menu online and pre-select what you will order. You will look decisive and serious when you don't have to hem and haw over your lunch choice.

Handling the utensils – In America, most are taught to hold the fork in the right hand, put it down to switch the knife into the right hand to cut then replace with the fork in the right hand again to raise a bite to the mouth. This, honestly, is a bit exhausting. Once you feel comfortable try the European style.

European style: Fork in the left hand, knife in the right. This is becoming much more common at American tables. It is definitely acceptable and in most cases considered more sophisticated. It does save a lot of utensil switching when you are in need of a lot of knife action.

Be Pleasant

Article Six: Be Pleasant

Nobody Cares About Your Bad Day. If
You're in a Mood, Stay Home.

Here we go. You are geared up for a
night out on the town, in a club or at a
friend's. You have gallantly finished the
work week and put away the daily
grind and myriad distractions that
comprise the lives we live. You are
ready to raise hell and enjoy a civilized
night out. You and your friends, or your
date, or what have you have gathered
on this great night, and the mood is
light with the promise of untold
amusements. Gaiety is afoot (no, I am
not afraid to use that word). Then in
walks Pigpen. You know the Peanuts'
character who walks around in a dirty
cloud? Yes, Pigpen walks in with his
bad mood and attempts to bring the
party down with him like some social
Chernobyl. On a weekend getaway to
my friend CDL's house in the Litchfield

County, Connecticut countryside last summer, I had the pleasure of attending a very nice dinner party. You know the routine by now. Tasty food, stimulating conversation, liberal libations, even an impromptu dance party after dinner all were in the cards. Oh, it was a grand time, I tell you, except for one annoying distraction: Pigpen. Evidently, Pigpen was in a snit with his companion over an argument so fresh from the oven it was still steaming. He stared intensely and scowled sourly at the other guests throughout dinner, drinks, even on the dance rug. He tried in earnest to bring the mood down to his level, but thank God, we, the rest of the party, were far too insistent to be persuaded. Any lesser souls would have succumbed to his attempt to ruin the night, but oh not we. This hearty band of merrymakers squashed him.

Now believe me. As sunshine and roses as I like to believe my personality to be, there are times when the black cloud descends even on this effervescent being. I know. And when I know, I stay home.

It is hard to believe, but it is true. And when this happens I respectfully decline an invitation. Who wants it? Not I, not the guests, certainly not the host. Leave your bad mood at home until the sun shines again and you can offer your best self to the world, not your worst. Good times can be hard to come by. Don't throw a wet blanket on the festivities. Stay at home and curl up in it instead.

❧ The Code ❧

☞ No one should know that someone is having relationship problems or is in a bad mood. This should be disguised from all but our closest friends and family.

☞ If you're in a bad mood, STAY HOME! If I've said it once, I've said it a thousand times: it is the responsibility of every single person at an event to contribute to that event's merriment.

Dance for your drinks and sing for your supper.

Compliment with Caution

Article Seven: Compliment with Caution

Yes, She's Gorgeous, But Keep a Lid on the Effusive Compliments.

Without giving too much away to make this point, SP will attempt this scenario. While flipping through the television channels recently, I landed on one of those fascinating/insipid reality show reunions and one element stood out so incredibly it has stuck in the craw. What could it be, you wonder, as those shows by nature run anathema to all we attempt here? Yes, forgetting the rude outbursts, name calling, inappropriate tears and far too intimate revelations, there was a civil violation that stood out above all the rest. And it was committed by the host! Now you know by now we hold a host in high regard and to an even higher standard, so this should come as no surprise.

As the host walked onto the set, he greeted one of the women with, "You look amazing!" And then went on, exclamation free, to the next one and the next one and the next one, never mentioning that the three others looked equally pulled together. Then to insult the injury, he landed on the last one to announce, "You look absolutely gorgeous!" There sat the other three having to listen to how gorgeous the other two were. It was shocking, I tell you. Why had these compliments offended? Well, like most of the things we don't like seeing in others' characteristics we first recognize in ourselves. Perhaps a shade of Freudian counter-transference? I must admit I have been a frequent employer of this terrible habit. It is always a spontaneous outburst that when I see a beautiful woman incredibly turned out, I want to let her know. I want to say, "You look incredible. Gorgeous. Thank you." And I have done this often and am afraid to say the outbursts increase with volume and effusion when I am in the cups. Well, it isn't until I saw this action displayed so vulgarly on the TV screen that I grasped how utterly insulting these assessments can be. And not to get too 12 Step on you, but, ahem. To all the women SP has insulted over the years, please accept this apology. I think you ALL look amazing. Well, to the ones who tried, that is. No apologies offered to women who wear sweatpants on airplanes. Sorry, I do have my limits. And standards.

There is an old-school rule when strict etiquette demanded what a man could and could not say to a woman he knew. Forget conversing or complimenting a woman to whom he had never been introduced: that would have been unthinkable. Oh, but yes, times have changed. We're much less formal and far more equal these days. This is a hard lesson to learn — especially for a Southerner prone to putting women on the (admittedly misogynistic) pedestal, but let's try our best to adjust to the times. So where does this leave us? I can't imagine any modern woman being insulted by a man commenting positively on her appearance (wolf whistling is not a positive comment), but that is one we will have to wait to hear from the ladies to know. As for commenting on one particular woman's appearance in the company of another women or group, this is unequivocally in bad taste, lacking decorum and full of all sorts of negative connotations. Don't do it. Bite your tongue.

– The Code –

☞ A compliment to one woman is an insult to the rest. Every woman within earshot has just heard you praise one woman's appearance over her own.

☞ To the woman receiving the outburst it may be taken as if she looks particularly good on this occasion with the implication being that she has looked less beautiful on other occasions.

☞ If you are so moved to comment on a woman's appearance, tell her discreetly (and not too leeringly or conspiratorially) and never within the earshot of others.

☞ If a solo woman approaches a group of men, the first to greet her should compliment her appearance with the rest of the men nodding politely but keeping quiet. There is no need for a gang bang of appreciation. Keep it cool. And appropriate.

దార్తీ

A Man Holds the Door

Article Eight: A Man Holds the Door

Hold the Door, Bro. Little Things equal Grand Gestures.

Gay, Straight, Bi or just curious, a man opens a door for a woman. We should be holding the door at all times so this practice becomes second nature. And this goes for car doors as well, mind you. Yes, we know this and we practice this on a first date or two, then lapse into a comfortable state and forget. In a nod to modernity, this rule can be relaxed when the sexes mix and it is all old friends and no romance, but always keep this courtesy handy and at the ready.

On a similar topic, a man driving a woman home walks her to the door. Exception to this rule would be when you are the same age or the girl is a younger cousin and she jumps out of the car before you can react or perhaps you are old friends and this formality seems, well, formal. At night a gentleman driving a car should always wait until his passenger is safely inside the house or building before pulling away. This courtesy should be extended to anyone actually, man or woman. If you are driving someone home or to a destination at night, wait for your passenger to walk safely through the door of their destination. As for city folks entertaining in high rises or apartment buildings, a gentleman should always walk a woman to a taxi. I have seen far too many a woman attempt to leave a party unescorted to the street. Even if she objects or refuses your offer, make up an excuse to run down to the corner deli for a pack of mints, and on the way you will safely deposit her into a taxi, feminism (and our shared civility) still intact.

❧ The Code ❦

☞ Open the car door for your mother, your aunt, your grandmother, for any woman your age or older.

☞ Front doors — any door you open — should be held to allow a woman to walk through before you. If it's an extremely heavy door you can push through before her and hold it until she passes.

☞ On a revolving door, give it a push to start the contraption moving then allow the lady to enter first. Alone. One person in a revolving-door pie slice at a time, please.

☞ A man walks behind a woman going up the stairs, in front of her on the way down.

☞ A man walks into a room before a woman if the room is dark or creepy. The general rule is that if the path is easy and clear, a woman leads. If it is dark, dangerous, crowded or unknown, a man leads. While we're at it, let's not see a man striding ahead of his woman. Walk side-by-side or slightly behind. Show some respect and deference.

 The hold-the-door-policy goes for older gentlemen as well. Younger defers to older as man defers to woman.

கூ

A Man Hugs the Curb

Article Nine: A Man Hugs the Curb

Although Runaway Horses and Mud-Splashing Autos Are Not Our Everyday Concerns, Stay on the Curb Side of Your Lady Friend.

There are few things that get under my skin more than witnessing a man walking with a woman on the sidewalk and the man not knowing or caring where he belongs. A man, or should I say, a *gentle* man, always walks on the street or curb side of the sidewalk in America (the Euro tradition states that a man walks on a woman's left, which can be curb side or building side.) As for the transgressors against this rule, I suspect the violators don't know any better and saunter on in oblivious bliss. It is no wonder that some men are confused because they have read or heard the opposing opinion that a gentleman walks on the building side. This alternate opinion is based on the notion that in the case that a flower pot or soup can should fall from a ledge or an open window and plunk his lady friend on the head, the gentleman would be there to catch said pot or at least absorb the brunt of the collision with his own thicker skull. The argument for the curbside is that a woman is protected from a wet or muddy splash caused by a passing car or a runaway horse or perhaps some ne'er do well looking for trouble.

A gentleman walks on the curb side of the sidewalk when walking with a woman. Basta. Of course, I understand that this can be a bit awkward when walking in a city such as New York, Boston, Charleston or San Francisco when a couple may encounter many turns and street crossings in a relatively short jaunt. In fact, I once had a lady friend say to me, "I know you are well-mannered and your intentions are gallant, but you are annoying the hell out me with all this switching from side to side." In this case I acknowledged (to myself) my mistake for making my action so ostentatious and vowed (to myself) to make my transitions smoother in the future. But the truth is I cannot enjoy the walk if I am not on the curb. It's so ingrained that it's damn near obsessive. Or is it compulsive? Whatever it is, I am content in my place and confident the majority of women appreciate the gesture.

❧ The Code ❧

☞A man walks on the curb side of a woman.

☞If in a run-down, sketchy or darkened area, the man should switch sides if there is a sense of insecurity, such as hidden alcoves, alley ways, a patch of ruffians, hooligans or out-of-control drunks.

Hang Up the Phone

Article Ten: Hang Up the Phone

Hang up the Damn Cell Phone &
Stop Texting at the Table.
You Are Not That Important.

One of my favorite summer places for cheap and cheerful eats is a little seaside snack shack on the Cape called Blue Light. The Blue Light is not fancy. It is not even a restaurant per se. There are no tables inside, only a couple of very stiff benches out front that discourage loitering and offer no shade from the scorching August sun. The food is excellent and very inexpensive. My point? This is not a fancy place. As for the establishment's attitude toward the cell-phone-rudeness epidemic, there is a sign on the counter that says it all: "We will gladly take your order when you have finished your cell phone conversation."

I have received many requests to address this plague and resisted – thus far — as the reach of this problem seemed too established to reverse, and frankly, I felt I could ignore the issue when it was confined to the Hollywood Tart set. Well, the plague has entered my world, and it must be addressed as recent events have shaken me from this complacency.

A very fine lady I know — let's call her Willa Winecup – regaled me with this story. Mrs. Winecup's sixteen year-old son has taken a girlfriend and said girlfriend was expected for dinner on a recent evening. Now my Mrs. Winecup was as excited — and apprehensive — as any mother would be to meet the new little lady in her son's life. On the appointed evening, the door bell rang, and Mrs. Winecup answered the door. What did she notice when she first laid eyes on the object of her son's affection? Her beauty? Her charm? Her dazzling smile or bright shiny hair? Well, no.

Little Lady was engrossed in a telephone call. Mrs. Winecup waited a few seconds to allow the girl to end the call and accept her welcome into her home. Little Lady barely acknowledged Mrs. Winecup but managed to lift a hold-on-a-sec finger showing no intention of ending the call. Mrs. Winecup politely closed the door in Little Lady's face and went back to her kitchen. Poor thing. Her fate was sealed with that one little finger.

Another tale: There is a very stylish man I know – we'll call him Mr. Flaunt — who is welcome at any event and in fact makes most events slide into gear when he arrives. I have noticed that Mr. Flaunt has started to make a habit of entering a party while in full-throated conversation on his cell phone. Into a private house! He enters elegantly, mind you, dressed to the nines and impeccably groomed, but with one accessory too many. The cell phone is glued to his ear. He enters, puts the other guest on hold and has even held up the now famous finger of pause to his host. Oh, no. Where to begin?

❧ The Code ❧

☞ Hang up the phone. End the call in the car, the sidewalk, the front porch, wherever.

☞ One should never enter a home on the phone, or let the door open while still on the phone. The call should end before the bell is rung. If by the rare chance the call is an emergency, one would inform the host and excuse himself to a private room.

☞ One would never stand in the middle of a group of people while talking on the phone. If I weren't such a big fan of civility, I wouldn't mind seeing someone pry the phone out of the offender's hand and toss the contraption into the toilet.

☞ As for receiving calls at the dinner table, private home or public restaurant, don't. The same goes for texting. One should not constantly check for texts at the dinner table. This constant checking the phone and responding is disrespectful to the host and to the company assembled at table. If it is a man's intention to telegraph to the people around him that they are of no importance to him, then by all means he should continue with this abominable behavior. He should not expect to be invited back again. If there is an emergency or he is a doctor on call, he should check discreetly and leave the room if he needs to respond.

☞ Business calls and we're-meeting-at-the-corner-bar texts do not constitute an emergency. To paraphrase the Blue Light, we will gladly welcome your company when you have finished your cell phone conversation

☞ Lose the Blue Tooth – These wireless contraptions are ridiculous when used in public. The wearer looks like a doofus who thinks he's too important to interact with real people. Not to mention, having a one-sided conversation in public is rude and distracting.

☞ Do not talk on the phone anywhere that the sound and decibel level of your voice will disturb others: train, plane, bus, elevator, park or playground. NO ONE wants to hear your conversation.

☞ Do not snap photos at the table, but if you must, NEVER use a flash in a restaurant. Yes, there are situations when you really want to take a picture just use discretion. Be quick about it. Avoid drawing attention or disturbing those around you.

☞ Do not constantly check Twitter, Instagram, SnapChat or Facebook at the table. A good habit to have? Put your device away at the dinner table. Do not set the device ON the table under any circumstance.

☞ And for Pete's sake, turn the ringer off. AND while at it, lose the irritating ring tones. Do you really want to hear dogs or ducks coming from your phone?

☞ Avoid using speaker phone in public. Again, if no one wants to hear your side of a conversation, we definitely don't want to hear the person you are talking bleating at us from your phone.

Evening Dress Code

For Evening Events: Weddings,
Formals,
Prom, Dances & Deb Balls.

❧ A Proper Dinner Suit (Tuxedo) ❧

Black jacket with peak lapels – Shawl
collar is an acceptable alternative but
never notch collar.

| Peak | Shawl | Notch |

*A white dinner jacket is appropriate from
Memorial Day to Labor Day or in a resort
climate any time.*

Black pants with black satin stripe.

White Tennis collar shirt is preferred but
Wing collar is certainly acceptable.
Pleats versus placket front. Placket front
reads more formal, but I do like both. I

111

find placket stands up better to sweaty dance moves.

Bow tie is black. Black tie means black tie. White tie is only ever worn with tails. Ever!

Braces (suspenders) are black or white and make this suit so much more comfortable. You're already strapped in like a baby seat, braces let you breathe.

Cummerbund – non-negotiable. No to the vest, not the best look in spite of the current trend.

A note about Prom and Greek Formals: here is the time when many a girl wants her date to match her dress. If this is the case, try if you must, but a better idea is to match the pochette (pocket square) and leave the tie and cummerbund alone and black.

Shoes are patent lace ups (or highly shined leather) or opera pumps (or slippers). Or velvet slippers, if you're daring.

Cuff links – Gold knots & studs or black and silver or silver-plate. Try to avoid whimsy.

Pochette (pocket square) should be white silk, but I do like red sometimes. Or here is your chance to match your date's dress, if you must.

Black silk socks that go to the knee. If you want to feel extra old school, go with the garters.

Never wear a watch with a Dinner Suit.

❧ The Dark Suit Alternative ❧

You can get away with wearing a dark suit, Navy or Black, if you don't want to spring for a Tuxedo.

Suit – Black or Navy, trim cut, 2- button, but if it's a 3 button, DO NOT button the top button. If 2 Button, leave the bottom button undone.

Shirt – Crisp white Point collar shirt, NOT a button down. And by crisp, we mean starched and ironed. It can or cannot be French Cuff, depending on your style and if you own a pair of cuff links. Do not make up cuff links. No paper clips, or binder clips (yes, I've seen both) or any other cute-sy to be clever contraption.

Tie – If you're going with a suit and not a Tuxedo, do not wear a bow tie. You should wear a long dark tie, preferably black if the suit is black, navy if the suit is navy.

Pochette – Here's where you can have a little fun. Go crazy with color.

Socks – should match the pant color.

Shoes – Should be black, preferably lace-ups, Never loafers.

Belt – should match the shoes.

❧ The Charleston Tuxedo ❦

*This should be your default uniform,
day or night when not in a suit.*

Navy Blazer – can be 2 button or double
breasted. Gold/Brass buttons or dark
plastic, avoid white or color here. It
should fit.

Shirt – should be white or pink point
collar, (avoid Banker Blue as you sweat
through blue). The shirt should be
starched, ironed and clean.

Tie – Bow tie or long tie – can be any
color you want. Make it lively!

Pants – khakis or gray flannels (in colder
temps) or crazy britches in mad color or
embroidered icons (in warmer weather).

Belt – Ribbon belt, needlepoint belt, or
embroidered belt, even brown leather
belt but definitely not black.

Shoes – loafers or saddle shoes or bucks, no socks.

❧ Final Note ❧

A man's jacket is ALWAYS buttoned when he stands. There is nothing worse than seeing photographs of men at formal functions with jacket wide open and white shirt blazing. (Unbutton once seated, you do have to breathe).

House Guest Rules

or How to Achieve Most-Favored Guest Status

Of all of the elements of living the good life that a man should master, being a good guest must surely rank at the top of that list. It matters not if you are invited to a tailgate party, church social, summer barbecue, destination wedding, beach or country house for the weekend, in your role as the good guest you should be gracious, grateful, considerate and above all entertaining. One of these fundamentals without the other is like driving a car with three wheels. And of all of these entertaining is the most important, particularly for a single man. If you are able to entertain your host and fit seamlessly into her dinner, event, or household, you will be invited back time and again. When a man achieves Most-Favored Guest status he will have his pick of invitations.

Let's say you have been lucky enough to be invited for a weekend getaway. We are not talking about some twelve-person, frat-boy share at the beach. You have received an invitation to a private house with a small party of friends or better yet, to a friend's parents' summer house. Being a house guest is a special privilege, and you should prepare for this privilege. There are stories of many a house guest whose true colors were revealed during a weekend in the country and whose name suddenly disappeared from the invitation list of not only his hostess but of all of her friends' lists as well. When you are a house guest, you must be ever vigil and on your best behavior and at all times cognizant that you are in someone's house, not a hotel and not your parents' house but in a friend's place. The rules for social survival are stricter here than those for any of the other scenarios of being a good guest.

❧ The Respectable Bag. Before you even get in the car or head down to the train station you should pack lightly and carry your things in a presentable bag. No host wants to see you stumbling through her door with loads of luggage or spilling out of plastic trash bags.

❧ The Hostess (or Host) Gift. You should bring a small gift for your host whether this is your first visit or your fiftieth. If you don't have time before you leave or would rather wait to shop while you are there, this is fine. It is nice to present something to your hostess that fits with her style and taste. If you are visiting a married couple you would bring one gift meant for the house.

❧ Don't Act Like a Guest. The most important rule of being a good house guest is never act like a guest. Do not arrive at someone's house acting as if you have checked into a luxury hotel.

No one is there to wait on you, unless of course there is a staff of servants, but this situation is unique (see *Tips for Service* below). Here are some things to consider while you are soaking up the hospitality. Offer to drive to the liquor store and fill the cabinet with liquors and mixers. Help prepare the dinner, set the table, clean up after and volunteer to do the dishes. Volunteer to make a simple dessert, or if you are worthless in a kitchen, stop by the famous bake shop in town and pick up an apple cobbler and vanilla ice cream.

🍃 Wear appropriate clothing. Assimilate to the style of your host. Do not come down to breakfast in your boxer shorts. Cover up with a robe or better yet throw on your khakis and a polo shirt. Wash your face and comb you hair while you are at it. Every gentleman should own one pair of nice pajamas to wear as a house guest.

🍃 Adjust to your host's schedule. If your host retires early, so do you. If your host rises early, you rise early, unless she specifically tells you otherwise. I am lucky that my hosts prefer long talks after midnight while sipping Scotch on the porch.

🍂 Know When to Go. Finally and most importantly, be wary of extending your stay. There is an old gift shop plaque I have seen in many a vacation home that says something to the effect, "If by late Sunday afternoon two drinks turn into three and we ask you to stay another night, please disregard this drunken sentiment and stick to your original plan." The polite host will sometimes offer — and in most cases an extra day is acceptable — but be extra sensitive to the household's mood. If you sense this is just a perfunctory invitation, hop on the next train and keep to your original plan.

🍂 Thank You Note. A thank you note is absolutely necessary. It does not matter if you picked up the thousand-dollar dinner bill on your last night. Always send a thank you note.

The point here should be clear. You should completely alter your schedule, behavior and expectations to that of your host. If you present yourself as entertaining, pleasant and trouble-free you should have a grand old time and head back to your life well-rested while running through the memory of a weekend well spent. Nobody ever said being a house guest was easy, in fact it can be downright draining sometimes, which is why you should refrain from making a habit of it.

❧ Tips for Service ❧

When you are staying with friends who have permanent, live-in household staff in the city, in the country or at the beach it is appropriate to tip these workers for services performed. These staffers have their normal duties of attending to the household plus the added burden of cleaning up after you. Especially if they make your bed, provide fresh towels and present breakfast and lunch every day. At the end of a trip, slide $10 for every day you were there into an envelope with a little note, "Thank you Matilda." If there is multiple staff you should leave multiple tips. Present the tip in separate envelopes to the cook and to the housekeepers. One side note: make this action discreet. I once made the mistake of offending a hostess when she discovered the tip to her staff. The misunderstanding in her mind was that her staff is taken care of by her, and my tip was offensive. To set the record straight, this hostess was misguided. One does indeed tip household staff. I stumbled by letting the hostess discover the tip in the first place. Hand the envelope directly to the staff or place it under an object that is impossible to miss.

❧ House Guests DO ❧

✦ offer to help and anticipate your host's needs.

✦ keep your room clean and bed made.

✦ Offer to replace or repair anything you break, lose or mishandle.

✦ strip the bed when you leave, fold and leave sheets on top of the bedspread.

❧ House Guests DON'T ❧

❦ act like a guest.

❦ invite friends over or be always on the road visiting others than your hosts.

❦ And finally, yes, it's a vacation, but it's not Spring Break in Cancun. Don't get blotto drunk and make a fool of yourself. As always, handle your liquor.

Thank You Note

Every man should have personalized correspondence cards to jot off a quick note now and then, but certainly always to thank a host, a gift giver, an interviewer or any act of kindness you would like to acknowledge in style. I say fire off mash notes without caution, the more the better.

The Card. Keep it simple. 4 ½ by 6 inch white or ivory cards in a suitable thickness will do. Stick with black, grey or navy embossed (thermal embossed is fine) name or monogram to start. If you are settled, have your *address only* printed on the back flap of the matching envelope. And ALWAYS write out full words in an address. No abbreviations, even for road, street, boulevard or the state. You can leave this off if you are not settled and unsure of your address for the foreseeable future. You may add an envelope liner if you want. It's more expensive, but the look is rich.

I am often asked, "What is the proper R.S.V.P. or Thank You when invited by email?" Good question. This is a confusing proposition in this day of email invitations — or God forbid, "evites" – but an important one. The answer is simple. One should answer an invitation in the manner it was received: a paper invitation requires a paper thank you; a telephoned invitation requires a telephoned thank you and finally, the host who texts, facebooks or emails an invitation should expect that method in thank you. Of course, written thank you notes are always appreciated and appropriate. *Usually*, I say because one should use caution when writing an overly enthusiastic note. You don't want to look like a bounder or a climber. An experienced host will detect bounding, and you will have defeated your purpose, which was to recognize your host's generosity and to endear your presence at her next event. You never want to look too eager. The key is to convey that you are an old hand at this and you appreciate her effort. Don't blow it.

> ❧ A sample of a Thank You note ❦

Dear Mrs. Clabberdobber,

It was so kind of you to include me in your dinner party. The meal was delicious and the company superb. I cannot remember a more enjoyable evening.

> Cordially,
> Cooper

❧R.S.V.P. when there's no reply card❦

Begin with

K. Cooper Ray accepts with pleasure (or regretfully declines) your kind invitation

(Then repeat what is written on the invitation)

to the Lowcountry Ball on Wednesday, November 23rd at eight o'clock.

How to Tie a Bow Tie

(Looking in the mirror)

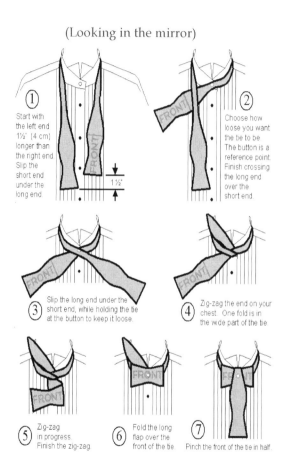

① Start with the left end 1½" (4 cm) longer than the right end. Slip the short end under the long end.

② Choose how loose you want the tie to be. The button is a reference point. Finish crossing the long end over the short end.

③ Slip the long end under the short end, while holding the tie at the button to keep it loose.

④ Zig-zag the end on your chest. One fold is in the wide part of the tie.

⑤ Zig-zag in progress. Finish the zig-zag.

⑥ Fold the long flap over the front of the tie.

⑦ Pinch the front of the tie in half.

131

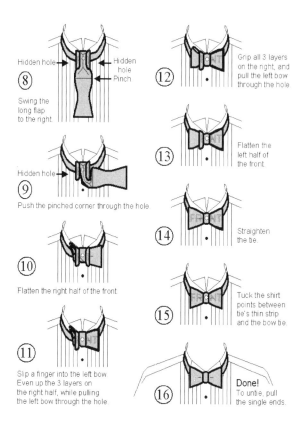

(8) Hidden hole → / ← Hidden hole / ← Pinch
Swing the long flap to the right.

(9) Hidden hole →
Push the pinched corner through the hole.

(10) Flatten the right half of the front.

(11) Slip a finger into the left bow. Even up the 3 layers on the right half, while pulling the left bow through the hole.

(12) Grip all 3 layers on the right, and pull the left bow through the hole.

(13) Flatten the left half of the front.

(14) Straighten the tie.

(15) Tuck the shirt points between tie's thin strip and the bow tie.

(16) Done! To untie, pull the single ends.

To achieve the signature Social Primer
contrasting bow, simply twist the single
tail & tighten knot.

Hat Rules

Whether baseball, beanie or top hat does not matter.

Take your hat off when you enter these situations.

🖌Entering a home, church, office, restaurant or theater.

🖌when the national anthem is played or the U.S. flag passes or is present.

🖌An old but awesomely respectful rule is that a man removes his hat when he passes a church.

A man does not remove his hat in these situations:

🖌Entering some public buildings (post office, airport, etc.), on public transportation or at athletic events.

☙in places where he remains standing: grocery stores or shops bars and coffee shops unless he sits, then the hat comes off.

☙when he passes through a building's hall or in the elevator.

-

138

The End.

Thank You.

❧❦

Contact

Mail: Post Office Box 872
            Charleston, South Carolina
            29401

Email: SP@socialprimer.com

Website: www.socialprimer.com

Facebook: Social Primer

Twitter: @socialprimer

Instagram: socialprimer